DEDICATION

This Reservations Book Log is dedicated to all the people out there who want to track their reservations and document their findings in the process.

You are my inspiration for producing books and I'm honored to be a part of keeping all of your random Reservations notes, and records organized.

This journal notebook will help you record your details about tracking your reservations.

Thoughtfully put together with these sections to record:

Day, Date, Time, # of People, Name, Phone Number, & Notes For Comments & Details.

HOW TO USE THIS BOOK

The purpose of this book is to keep all of your Reservations notes all in one place. It will help keep you organized.

This Reservations journal log will allow you to accurately document every detail about all of your Reservations. It's a great way to chart your course through organizing all your Reservations.

Here are examples of the prompts for you to fill in and write about your experience in this book:

- 31 Slots Per Page

- 5 Columns

- Day, Date

- Time

- Number Of People

- Name

- Phone

- Notes For Comments & Details

TIME	#PPL	NAME	PHONE	COMMENTS

TIME	#PPL	NAME	PHONE	COMMENTS

TIME	#PPL	NAME	PHONE	COMMENTS

TIME	#PPL	NAME	PHONE	COMMENTS

TIME	#PPL	NAME	PHONE	COMMENTS

TIME	#PPL	NAME	PHONE	COMMENTS

TIME	#PPL	NAME	PHONE	COMMENTS

TIME	#PPL	NAME	PHONE	COMMENTS

TIME	#PPL	NAME	PHONE	COMMENTS

TIME	#PPL	NAME	PHONE	COMMENTS

TIME	#PPL	NAME	PHONE	COMMENTS

TIME	#PPL	NAME	PHONE	COMMENTS

TIME	#PPL	NAME	PHONE	COMMENTS

TIME	#PPL	NAME	PHONE	COMMENTS

TIME	#PPL	NAME	PHONE	COMMENTS

TIME	#PPL	NAME	PHONE	COMMENTS

TIME	#PPL	NAME	PHONE	COMMENTS

TIME	#PPL	NAME	PHONE	COMMENTS

TIME	#PPL	NAME	PHONE	COMMENTS

TIME	#PPL	NAME	PHONE	COMMENTS

TIME	#PPL	NAME	PHONE	COMMENTS

TIME	#PPL	NAME	PHONE	COMMENTS

TIME	#PPL	NAME	PHONE	COMMENTS

TIME	#PPL	NAME	PHONE	COMMENTS

TIME	#PPL	NAME	PHONE	COMMENTS

TIME	#PPL	NAME	PHONE	COMMENTS

TIME	#PPL	NAME	PHONE	COMMENTS

TIME	#PPL	NAME	PHONE	COMMENTS

TIME	#PPL	NAME	PHONE	COMMENTS

TIME	#PPL	NAME	PHONE	COMMENTS

TIME	#PPL	NAME	PHONE	COMMENTS

TIME	#PPL	NAME	PHONE	COMMENTS

TIME	#PPL	NAME	PHONE	COMMENTS

TIME	#PPL	NAME	PHONE	COMMENTS

TIME	#PPL	NAME	PHONE	COMMENTS

TIME	#PPL	NAME	PHONE	COMMENTS

TIME	#PPL	NAME	PHONE	COMMENTS

TIME	#PPL	NAME	PHONE	COMMENTS

TIME	#PPL	NAME	PHONE	COMMENTS

TIME	#PPL	NAME	PHONE	COMMENTS

TIME	#PPL	NAME	PHONE	COMMENTS

TIME	#PPL	NAME	PHONE	COMMENTS

TIME	#PPL	NAME	PHONE	COMMENTS

TIME	#PPL	NAME	PHONE	COMMENTS

TIME	#PPL	NAME	PHONE	COMMENTS

TIME	#PPL	NAME	PHONE	COMMENTS

TIME	#PPL	NAME	PHONE	COMMENTS

TIME	#PPL	NAME	PHONE	COMMENTS

TIME	#PPL	NAME	PHONE	COMMENTS

TIME	#PPL	NAME	PHONE	COMMENTS

TIME	#PPL	NAME	PHONE	COMMENTS

TIME	#PPL	NAME	PHONE	COMMENTS

TIME	#PPL	NAME	PHONE	COMMENTS

TIME	#PPL	NAME	PHONE	COMMENTS

TIME	#PPL	NAME	PHONE	COMMENTS

TIME	#PPL	NAME	PHONE	COMMENTS

TIME	#PPL	NAME	PHONE	COMMENTS

TIME	#PPL	NAME	PHONE	COMMENTS

TIME	#PPL	NAME	PHONE	COMMENTS

TIME	#PPL	NAME	PHONE	COMMENTS

TIME	#PPL	NAME	PHONE	COMMENTS

TIME	#PPL	NAME	PHONE	COMMENTS

TIME	#PPL	NAME	PHONE	COMMENTS

TIME	#PPL	NAME	PHONE	COMMENTS

TIME	#PPL	NAME	PHONE	COMMENTS

TIME	#PPL	NAME	PHONE	COMMENTS

TIME	#PPL	NAME	PHONE	COMMENTS

TIME	#PPL	NAME	PHONE	COMMENTS

TIME	#PPL	NAME	PHONE	COMMENTS

TIME	#PPL	NAME	PHONE	COMMENTS

TIME	#PPL	NAME	PHONE	COMMENTS

TIME	#PPL	NAME	PHONE	COMMENTS

TIME	#PPL	NAME	PHONE	COMMENTS

TIME	#PPL	NAME	PHONE	COMMENTS

TIME	#PPL	NAME	PHONE	COMMENTS

TIME	#PPL	NAME	PHONE	COMMENTS

TIME	#PPL	NAME	PHONE	COMMENTS

TIME	#PPL	NAME	PHONE	COMMENTS

		Day/Date		
TIME	#PPL	NAME	PHONE	COMMENTS

TIME	#PPL	NAME	PHONE	COMMENTS

TIME	#PPL	NAME	PHONE	COMMENTS

TIME	#PPL	NAME	PHONE	COMMENTS

TIME	#PPL	NAME	PHONE	COMMENTS

TIME	#PPL	NAME	PHONE	COMMENTS

TIME	#PPL	NAME	PHONE	COMMENTS

TIME	#PPL	NAME	PHONE	COMMENTS

TIME	#PPL	NAME	PHONE	COMMENTS

TIME	#PPL	NAME	PHONE	COMMENTS

TIME	#PPL	NAME	PHONE	COMMENTS

TIME	#PPL	NAME	PHONE	COMMENTS

TIME	#PPL	NAME	PHONE	COMMENTS

TIME	#PPL	NAME	PHONE	COMMENTS

TIME	#PPL	NAME	PHONE	COMMENTS

TIME	#PPL	NAME	PHONE	COMMENTS

TIME	#PPL	NAME	PHONE	COMMENTS

TIME	#PPL	NAME	PHONE	COMMENTS

TIME	#PPL	NAME	PHONE	COMMENTS

TIME	#PPL	NAME	PHONE	COMMENTS

TIME	#PPL	NAME	PHONE	COMMENTS

TIME	#PPL	NAME	PHONE	COMMENTS

TIME	#PPL	NAME	PHONE	COMMENTS

TIME	#PPL	NAME	PHONE	COMMENTS

TIME	#PPL	NAME	PHONE	COMMENTS

TIME	#PPL	NAME	PHONE	COMMENTS

TIME	#PPL	NAME	PHONE	COMMENTS

TIME	#PPL	NAME	PHONE	COMMENTS

TIME	#PPL	NAME	PHONE	COMMENTS

TIME	#PPL	NAME	PHONE	COMMENTS

TIME	#PPL	NAME	PHONE	COMMENTS

TIME	#PPL	NAME	PHONE	COMMENTS

TIME	#PPL	NAME	PHONE	COMMENTS

TIME	#PPL	NAME	PHONE	COMMENTS

TIME	#PPL	NAME	PHONE	COMMENTS

TIME	#PPL	NAME	PHONE	COMMENTS

TIME	#PPL	NAME	PHONE	COMMENTS

TIME	#PPL	NAME	PHONE	COMMENTS

TIME	#PPL	NAME	PHONE	COMMENTS

TIME	#PPL	NAME	PHONE	COMMENTS

TIME	#PPL	NAME	PHONE	COMMENTS

TIME	#PPL	NAME	PHONE	COMMENTS

TIME	#PPL	NAME	PHONE	COMMENTS

TIME	#PPL	NAME	PHONE	COMMENTS

TIME	#PPL	NAME	PHONE	COMMENTS

TIME	#PPL	NAME	PHONE	COMMENTS

TIME	#PPL	NAME	PHONE	COMMENTS

TIME	#PPL	NAME	PHONE	COMMENTS

TIME	#PPL	NAME	PHONE	COMMENTS

TIME	#PPL	NAME	PHONE	COMMENTS

TIME	#PPL	NAME	PHONE	COMMENTS

TIME	#PPL	NAME	PHONE	COMMENTS

TIME	#PPL	NAME	PHONE	COMMENTS

TIME	#PPL	NAME	PHONE	COMMENTS

TIME	#PPL	NAME	PHONE	COMMENTS

Day/Date

TIME	#PPL	NAME	PHONE	COMMENTS

TIME	#PPL	NAME	PHONE	COMMENTS

TIME	#PPL	NAME	PHONE	COMMENTS

TIME	#PPL	NAME	PHONE	COMMENTS

TIME	#PPL	NAME	PHONE	COMMENTS

TIME	#PPL	NAME	PHONE	COMMENTS

TIME	#PPL	NAME	PHONE	COMMENTS

TIME	#PPL	NAME	PHONE	COMMENTS

TIME	#PPL	NAME	PHONE	COMMENTS

TIME	#PPL	NAME	PHONE	COMMENTS

TIME	#PPL	NAME	PHONE	COMMENTS

TIME	#PPL	NAME	PHONE	COMMENTS

TIME	#PPL	NAME	PHONE	COMMENTS

TIME	#PPL	NAME	PHONE	COMMENTS

TIME	#PPL	NAME	PHONE	COMMENTS

TIME	#PPL	NAME	PHONE	COMMENTS

TIME	#PPL	NAME	PHONE	COMMENTS

TIME	#PPL	NAME	PHONE	COMMENTS

TIME	#PPL	NAME	PHONE	COMMENTS

TIME	#PPL	NAME	PHONE	COMMENTS

TIME	#PPL	NAME	PHONE	COMMENTS

TIME	#PPL	NAME	PHONE	COMMENTS

TIME	#PPL	NAME	PHONE	COMMENTS

TIME	#PPL	NAME	PHONE	COMMENTS

TIME	#PPL	NAME	PHONE	COMMENTS

TIME	#PPL	NAME	PHONE	COMMENTS

TIME	#PPL	NAME	PHONE	COMMENTS

TIME	#PPL	NAME	PHONE	COMMENTS

TIME	#PPL	NAME	PHONE	COMMENTS

TIME	#PPL	NAME	PHONE	COMMENTS

TIME	#PPL	NAME	PHONE	COMMENTS

TIME	#PPL	NAME	PHONE	COMMENTS

TIME	#PPL	NAME	PHONE	COMMENTS

Day/Date				
TIME	#PPL	NAME	PHONE	COMMENTS

TIME	#PPL	NAME	PHONE	COMMENTS

TIME	#PPL	NAME	PHONE	COMMENTS

TIME	#PPL	NAME	PHONE	COMMENTS

TIME	#PPL	NAME	PHONE	COMMENTS

TIME	#PPL	NAME	PHONE	COMMENTS

TIME	#PPL	NAME	PHONE	COMMENTS

TIME	#PPL	NAME	PHONE	COMMENTS

TIME	#PPL	NAME	PHONE	COMMENTS

TIME	#PPL	NAME	PHONE	COMMENTS

TIME	#PPL	NAME	PHONE	COMMENTS

TIME	#PPL	NAME	PHONE	COMMENTS

TIME	#PPL	NAME	PHONE	COMMENTS

TIME	#PPL	NAME	PHONE	COMMENTS

TIME	#PPL	NAME	PHONE	COMMENTS

TIME	#PPL	NAME	PHONE	COMMENTS

TIME	#PPL	NAME	PHONE	COMMENTS

TIME	#PPL	NAME	PHONE	COMMENTS

TIME	#PPL	NAME	PHONE	COMMENTS

TIME	#PPL	NAME	PHONE	COMMENTS

TIME	#PPL	NAME	PHONE	COMMENTS

TIME	#PPL	NAME	PHONE	COMMENTS

TIME	#PPL	NAME	PHONE	COMMENTS

TIME	#PPL	NAME	PHONE	COMMENTS

TIME	#PPL	NAME	PHONE	COMMENTS

TIME	#PPL	NAME	PHONE	COMMENTS

TIME	#PPL	NAME	PHONE	COMMENTS

TIME	#PPL	NAME	PHONE	COMMENTS

TIME	#PPL	NAME	PHONE	COMMENTS

TIME	#PPL	NAME	PHONE	COMMENTS

TIME	#PPL	NAME	PHONE	COMMENTS

TIME	#PPL	NAME	PHONE	COMMENTS

TIME	#PPL	NAME	PHONE	COMMENTS

TIME	#PPL	NAME	PHONE	COMMENTS

TIME	#PPL	NAME	PHONE	COMMENTS

TIME	#PPL	NAME	PHONE	COMMENTS

TIME	#PPL	NAME	PHONE	COMMENTS

TIME	#PPL	NAME	PHONE	COMMENTS

TIME	#PPL	NAME	PHONE	COMMENTS

TIME	#PPL	NAME	PHONE	COMMENTS

TIME	#PPL	NAME	PHONE	COMMENTS

TIME	#PPL	NAME	PHONE	COMMENTS

TIME	#PPL	NAME	PHONE	COMMENTS

TIME	#PPL	NAME	PHONE	COMMENTS

TIME	#PPL	NAME	PHONE	COMMENTS

TIME	#PPL	NAME	PHONE	COMMENTS

TIME	#PPL	NAME	PHONE	COMMENTS

TIME	#PPL	NAME	PHONE	COMMENTS

TIME	#PPL	NAME	PHONE	COMMENTS

TIME	#PPL	NAME	PHONE	COMMENTS

TIME	#PPL	NAME	PHONE	COMMENTS

TIME	#PPL	NAME	PHONE	COMMENTS

TIME	#PPL	NAME	PHONE	COMMENTS

TIME	#PPL	NAME	PHONE	COMMENTS